FIREARMS IN AMERICAN HISTORY

MICHAEL L. BERGER

FIREARMS IN AMERICAN HISTORY

Franklin Watts
New York / London / 1979
A First Book

Photographs courtesy of:

Colonial Williamsburg Foundation: frontispiece, pp. 12–13, 54 (top left and right and bottom right); State Department of Archives and History, Raleigh, N.C., p. 2; Library of Congress: pp. 6, 16; New York Public Library Picture Collection: pp. 21, 27, 34, 40 (right), 46; National Archives: p. 30; Denver Public Library, Western Collection: p. 40 (left); Remington Arms Company, Inc.: pp. 47, 54 (bottom left).

Art by Vantage Art, Inc.

Library of Congress Cataloging in Publication Data

Berger, Michael.
    Firearms in American history.

    (A First book)
    Bibliography: p.
    Includes index.
    SUMMARY: Highlights the history of firearms from their appearance in Europe in the 14th century through the settling of America and the Civil War. Discusses firearms in sport and competition and the art of gunsmithing.
    1. Firearms—United States—Juvenile literature. 2. United States—History—Juvenile literature. [1. Firearms—History] I. Title.
TS533.2.B47   683'.4   78-11652
ISBN 0-531-02255-2

CONTENTS

In Memory of
Linda's Parents

The history of technology is a complex field, one in which no individual can hope to make a contribution without help from others. In the writing of this volume, I was fortunate to receive the assistance and cooperation of a number of people.

Gary Brumfield, Master Gunsmith at Colonial Williamsburg, and Etta Falkner, Librarian at Old Sturbridge Village, provided valuable bibliographic information. Mary Stone and her colleagues at the St. Mary's College of Maryland Library performed yeoman service in securing books and articles for my research. Burt Kummerow of the St. Mary's City Commission read an early draft of the manuscript and made valuable suggestions for improving it.

I owe a special debt of gratitude to my editor at Franklin Watts, Maury Solomon. It was she who originally interested me in this project, helped provide both boundaries and direction to my research, and improved immeasurably the form and style of the writing herein.

Ultimately, however, it was the understanding and wise counsel of my wife, Linda, which allowed me to continue my writing during a period of rapid change for us both.

CHAPTER

A PERFECT TOOL
FOR SETTLEMENT

So significant were firearms to early American history that one writer has claimed, "Firearms, the axe, and the plow were the three cornerstones upon which the pioneer Americans built this nation."

When the European settlers began to arrive in North America in the seventeenth century, they found an immense area of relatively untouched land and incredibly abundant supplies of wild game, fish, and fruits. The firearm was to become one of the most important tools for settling this new land.

It is difficult for us today to imagine the tremendous numbers and variety of game that populated America early in its history. As late as 1808, huge flocks of passenger pigeons—containing perhaps millions of birds each—were still being reported. *Single* herds of over 500,000 buffalo still roamed the Great Plains. So numerous were birds and animals that, in addition to being killed for practical reasons, they were also shot just for practice and sport. American wildlife seemed boundless.

Hunting became a chief occupation of the early settlers. Skill in hunting, and the firearms that made such skill possible, provided an easy way to kill the wild animals that roamed across the land and the birds that literally blackened the sky. Settlers were thus able to secure for themselves a large supply of meat, to supplement the vegetables and fruits they were able to grow and gather. According to one historian, the Massachusetts pilgrims "astounded" the native Indians by being able to bring down crows in flight. The Indians had never seen firearms before this.

By using even the crude weapons of the day, it was possible for anyone, with just the least bit of industry, to secure enough meat to eat and enough hides for clothing. The mainstay of the colonists' diet was the wild turkey, which liked to live in treeless areas and thus happily nested near settlements, where it was easily shot. So popular did the turkey become that it was later suggested to serve as the national bird, and is still the main dish at most traditional American holiday meals.

Hunting with firearms also made possible the production of goods that could be traded abroad. Animal hides, more specifically, furs, were such goods. In European cities, there grew up an increasing demand for deerskins, bearskins, buffalo robes, and the like. It was the musket and the rifle that allowed the colonists, and later Americans moving westward, to supply this demand.

The fur trapper, with his musket,
provided early America with
goods that could be sold abroad.

Most men hunted only to supply their own needs and those of their families. Some, however, tried to kill more animals than they needed, so that they could sell the extra furs or meat for a profit. Unlike the individual settler, who hunted for a day or so at a time, the "professional" frequently spent several days and sometimes weeks at his task. He would take with him a large supply of ammunition, probably several different firearms, materials and tools to repair his weapons should something go wrong, and related gear.

Firearms also provided the settlers with a means of protecting themselves. Unfriendly Indians, angered by the loss of their land and game, would sometimes attack the colonists or destroy the colonists' property in attempts to discourage further settlement.

In addition, livestock and crops—even the settlers themselves—were in constant danger from predators. Bears, wolves, and wildcats could be troublesome enemies. Occasionally, groups would be organized aimed at ridding the area of some nuisance. Such "animal drives" reached the height of their popularity in the mid-eighteenth century. One such drive in Pennsylvania around 1760 involved approximately two hundred hunters, who formed a circle and gradually closed it, in an attempt to kill the panthers and wolves that had been preying on neighborhood livestock. The toll of this drive indicates again the abundance of wildlife at the time: 41 panthers, 109 wolves, 112 foxes, 114 mountain cats, 17 black bears, 1 white bear, 2 elk, 198 deer, 111 buffalo, 3 fishers, 1 otter, 12 gluttons, 3 beavers, and 500 additional smaller animals were killed.

Finally, in times of war, it was the responsibility of all

able-bodied men to shoulder arms when called upon. While frequently the weapons used and the ammunition for them was stored in a central location such as the blockhouse, just as often the militiaman was expected to supply his own gun, powder, and shot. Sometimes these two practices were combined, with the colony purchasing primarily military weapons (muskets), and the citizen expected to bring his hunting gun (often a rifle) as well.

Thus firearms were considered a necessity in early America. They were tools to be used when the occasion warranted it, and skill in their operation was almost automatically passed on to the next generation. The necessity for skillful use of firearms by private citizens continued down into much of the nineteenth century, especially in the frontier portion of the United States. Not surprisingly, an English visitor at the time of the Revolutionary War commented, "There is not a Man born in America that does not understand the Use of Firearms and that well. . . . It is almost the First thing they Purchase and take to all the New Settlements and in the Cities you can scarcely find a Lad of 12 years That does not go a Gunning. . . ."

It might well be noted here that the colonists were not the only firearm users in America. Those Indians whom the Europeans found living along the coast were primarily a hunting and fishing people. They depended on these undertakings and on a limited amount of farming to provide not only food, but clothing and shelter as well. Their main weapon had been the bow and arrow, and there is much evidence to indicate that until well into the eighteenth century, this weapon was superior to shoulder arms in accuracy, effectiveness, and speed of handling. None-

theless, thanks mostly to the strong encouragement of the settlers, firearms gradually came to replace the bow and arrow in the Indian way of life.

The introduction of firearms to the native American tribes profoundly changed their way of life. Indians with guns began to attack those without, sometimes to steal valuable furs and pelts. As hunting with a gun made killing a relatively safe, impersonal activity that could be successfully accomplished by nearly anyone, Indians had to redefine for themselves what was meant by bravery and strength.

Though the firearm replaced the bow and arrow for the Indians, the Indians never really developed the ability to build their own firearms or to repair major defects in those that they owned. As a result, they became dependent on the settlers for their supply of guns and for the weapons' upkeep, and the only way they could secure these things was by killing more of the game that formerly had made them economically independent. A vicious circle had been created from which the Indians were never to escape.

The weapons that were brought to America from Europe soon proved inadequate; they had been intended for different environments and different life-styles. In the years ahead, Americans would first modify European weapons and then invent totally new types to fit their unique needs. In the chapters that follow, we will look at some of these changes.

The militia of colonial America.

CHAPTER

THE EARLY HISTORY
OF FIREARMS

Firearms first appeared in Europe in the fourteenth century. The earliest models were simply iron tubes with one end sealed off and a small hole drilled into a side near the closed end. A measure of explosive powder was poured down the opening, followed by some type of projectile (a piece of metal, a stone, or any small, solid object). Fire could then be applied to the side hole, thereby igniting the powder, and the force of the explosion would push the projectile out of the open end of the iron tube.

Admittedly, these were very primitive weapons. Yet they contained within them the basic elements that define all firearms even today. Specifically, there is a "barrel" (the tube) into which "ammunition" (the explosive mixture and the bullet or shot pellet) is placed. Then, a mechanical firing device (the "lock") is set in motion by pulling a "trigger," and the resulting explosion expels the bullet or shot out through the barrel. To aid in holding this weapon and to provide some protection from the barrel, which was likely to heat up and recoil when fired, a

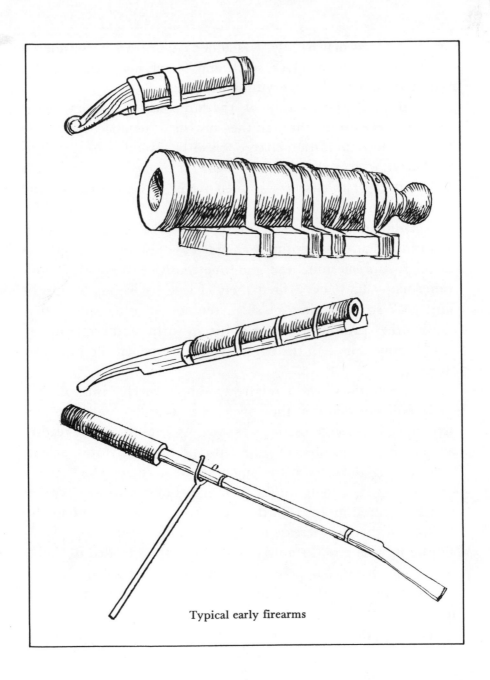

Typical early firearms

"stock," or wooden handle, was added. A firearm is considered complete when it has a lock, stock, and barrel; hence the popular phrase indicating that everything is present.

Up until the middle of the nineteenth century, most firearms were loaded through the "muzzle," the open end of the barrel. The ammunition charge was either simply dropped into the barrel, with gravity doing the work, or pushed into place with a "ramrod." The charge was then ready to be ignited by the action of the lock.

Although there were several types of locks invented between 1350 and 1650, one eventually emerged as most popular, and was to reign supreme until the mid-nineteenth century. Flint ignition locks—"flintlocks"—fired their charge by having a chip of flint rock strike a piece of steel, thereby creating sparks that ignited the "priming" powder. This, in turn, fired the gunpowder through a hole in the barrel, which propelled the bullet or shot out.

The flintlock was a relatively simple mechanism, all but foolproof provided that the powder was kept dry, and inexpensive in comparison to earlier weapons. As a result, it was readily adaptable to a number of different-type firearms. Most prominent among these were the smoothbore musket, which today would be called a shotgun; the American Long or Kentucky rifle, which featured grooves inside the barrel to give a spin to the bullet and thereby increase its accuracy; and a single-shot pistol, similar in nature to the musket but obviously intended for holding in one's hand, as opposed to resting on one's shoulder.

Beginning in the mid-nineteenth century, firearms inventors began to produce practical breech-loading weapons. The "breech" is that point where the rear of the barrel meets the stock. Although the lock had always been located there, and it was realized that insertion of the ammunition at that point would greatly simplify loading, it took a considerable period of experimentation to achieve a successful model. The breech-loading process was adapted to the three types of weapons mentioned above, and eventually made possible a fourth one—the "repeating," or multiple-shot firearm.

Most of the early shoulder arms imported into the American colonies were of the smoothbore variety. When this weapon was fired, the bullet or shot, being smaller than the bore (the diameter of the barrel), literally ricocheted its way down the barrel, finally exiting in a somewhat random direction. Obviously, with such poor accuracy, these guns were really only useful when the enemy or the game appeared in large groups, so that a shot in the general area would do some damage. Even then, if the target were more than 100 yards (91.4 m) away, there was little chance of hitting it.

A different type of arm—the rifle—seemed to hold more promise if it could be modified for the American way of life. Rifles differed from smoothbore muskets in that they had grooves ("rifling" marks) cut on the inside of the barrel, and fired a lead ball large enough to fit snugly inside. When the ball was expelled by the force of the gunpowder explosion, it was made to spin by the rifling, and thus was able to achieve greater stability, accuracy, range, and impact.

The rifle had been the brainchild of the Germans and the Swiss in Europe. It was somewhat logical, therefore, that people descended from these same nationalities in America would be the ones who would alter the rifle to better suit the new-world experience. To begin with, they narrowed the bore, thus decreas-

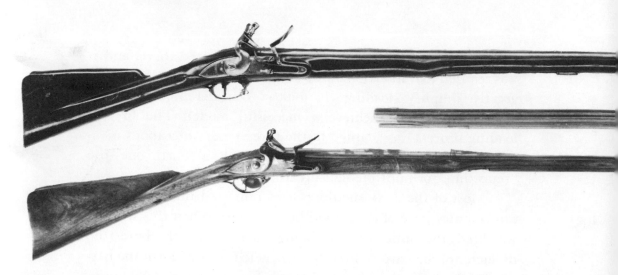

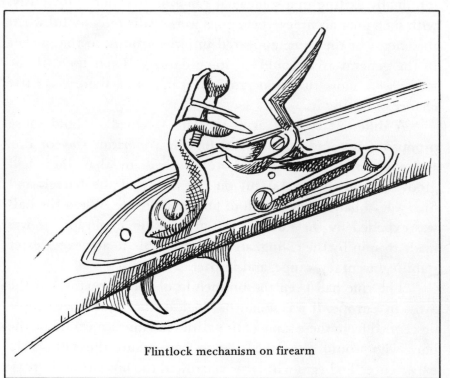

Flintlock mechanism on firearm

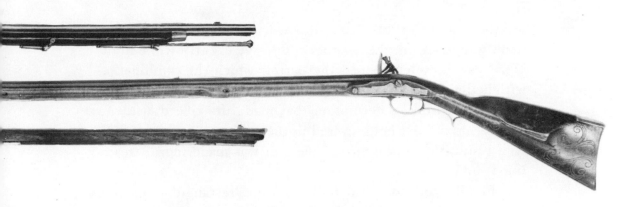

Top: a Brown Bess musket, made in 1760.
Middle: a Kentucky rifle, dating back to 1774.
Bottom: an English flintlock fowling piece, made in 1753.

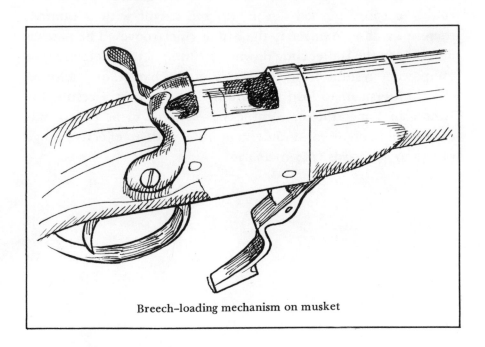

Breech–loading mechanism on musket

ing the amount of lead and gunpowder needed. Both of these items were scarce in the colonies and heavy to carry while hunting. Next, they lengthened the barrel, which, in combination with better aiming sights, improved the accuracy of the weapon. Then, all European decoration that made the rifle difficult to handle and did not hold up well in the wilderness was removed. As a result, the appearance of the gun was made more streamlined and functional.

Finally, the stock had built into it a rectangular opening approximately 5 by 1½ inches (12.7 cm by 3.9 cm), which was then covered with a hinged brass, wood, or iron lid. This "patch box" could be used by the shooter to stash a supply of greased buckskin patches. By making the ball slightly smaller than the bore, and wrapping it in one of these greased patches, it could be easily pushed down into the barrel with a ramrod, thereby avoiding damage to the ball or rifle grooves. The patches also helped the bullet slide down the rifling better, helped clean gunpowder residue from the inside of the barrel, and allowed the frontiersman to load and fire in less time. As a result, the American Long rifle, or Kentucky as it came to be called, was capable of being fired in under a minute, with an effective range of 150 to 300 yards (137 to 274 m).

CHAPTER

3

FIREARMS IN THE REVOLUTIONARY WAR

The colonists' concern and skill with firearms was a decided advantage to the American cause during the Revolutionary War. It is no accident that the famous statue on Lexington Green in Massachusetts, which commemorates the start of the Revolution, refers to the "shot heard 'round the world." As historian Philipe Sharpe has correctly observed, America "was born with the rifle in its hand."

Surprisingly, the smoothbore, flintlock musket was used by both sides during most of the military encounters that took place in the war. Why was this true when the rifle seemed to be a superior weapon? For one thing, most battles of that period involved large numbers of troops lined up across from each other. In such a situation, accuracy was less important than firepower, and the musket could be loaded and fired three times quicker than a rifle. In addition, the tremendous amount of smoke sent up by the black gunpowder used in rifles at that time would have made it difficult to aim at a specific target even

Battles of the Revolutionary War period usually involved the use of muskets with bayonets attached.

if a soldier wanted to. Furthermore, rifles were not made with bayonets, and this was a real disadvantage given the way battles were fought at this time. Hand-to-hand bayonet fighting, which followed the shooting of a few introductory rounds of ammunition, was still considered the most effective way to defeat an enemy. And last, but certainly not least, the rifle was a costlier weapon to produce. The new nation had enough trouble raising money from the former colonies without asking for the additional revenue necessary to arm the troops with rifles.

Even though the smoothbore musket was the weapon favored by military leaders, the rifle did come to play an important role in the war too. In 1775, Congress financed the formation of ten rifle companies. American riflemen, using a combination of military-made rifles and personal weapons brought from home, increasingly began to serve as snipers and sharpshooters, firing at and weakening the advancing British forces prior to the main battle.

These guerrilla-like tactics were a contributing factor to the eventual success of the American cause. The British, hearing reports of many of their finest officers being shot by rifles from distances of 200 to 300 yards (183 to 274 m), grew disheartened. Such distance and accuracy was unheard of with a musket. In 1775, the Bradford brothers of Philadelphia, two printers who remained loyal to England throughout the war, wrote a letter to a friend abroad that was published in a London newspaper and that read, in part, "This Province [Pennsylvania] has raised 1000 riflemen, the worst of whom will put a ball into a man's head at a distance of 150 or 200 yards [137 or 183 m]. Therefore advise your officers who shall hereafter come out to America to settle their affairs in England before their departure."

Although the British were never able to completely equal the superior American marksmanship, they did employ rifles themselves, at least indirectly. The Jäger rifle, from which the Kentucky was developed, was used by the German Hessians, mercenary soldiers who were paid to fight for the British. Fortunately for American independence, the Jäger was not as accurate as the Kentucky rifle, nor was the Hessian commitment to their cause as strong as that of the Americans who were fighting for their freedom, families, and land.

By the war's end, the superiority of the rifle in many respects had been shown. Although not yet a perfect military weapon, further refinements would make it so. While military leaders would be slow in accepting it, the disappearance of the musket was just a matter of time. This sequence of events, in which a war is responsible for technical advances in weaponry, is a theme that continues throughout American history.

CHAPTER

THE GUN MOVES WESTWARD WITH THE PIONEERS

Having so recently fought for their freedom from a tyrannical government, Americans were not about to give up the right to arm themselves or the right to overthrow the new federal government should it endanger their newfound liberties. Therefore the Bill of Rights, which were the first ten amendments added to the Constitution, were made to contain a guarantee that the citizens' right to bear arms would not be infringed upon. The wording of this amendment is such that one can interpret it in several different ways. Although it was probably intended to refer simply to the right of states to raise and maintain civilian militias, it soon became interpreted as an *individual* liberty, one which was vigorously exercised as Americans moved westward.

As the white population began to fill in the area east of the Mississippi River, those Indians that had withdrawn there from the Atlantic coast became somewhat of a "problem": they were occupying lands wanted by the pioneers. By the early 1800s, talk of "Indian removal" was gaining in popularity. Hoping to avoid bloodshed, the U.S. government adopted a policy better calculated to delay rather than to solve the problem. Contracts were signed for the production of a special weapon, variously called the Northwest, trade, or Indian gun, which would be available to Indians at trading posts in the unsettled regions in exchange for furs. The advantages of this policy were twofold. First, it provided for a continuation of the profitable fur trade that had been going on with Europe. Second, it offered the Indians a livelihood at the very time that their most valuable land was being absorbed by American pioneers. In fact, the Indians were often induced to sell or move off their lands by the offer of only firearms as a payment. As one example, in 1830 the government concluded a treaty with the Choctaw tribe providing a rifle, ammunition, and related gear to each warrior who would move west of the Mississippi River. This practice of buying off the Indians continued for another half-century.

Since these trade guns were sold by the federal government, Indians were allowed to come to selected forts to have their weapons repaired when necessary. To keep such expenses to a minimum, the trade gun was designed to be a comparatively simple weapon, easy and cheap both to manufacture and to fix. It was a smoothbore musket, which from the Indian perspective was good. Fine shot could be used to kill small game, while the gun could also be loaded with a musket ball for shooting larger animals and one's enemies.

Even as the Ohio Valley was being settled, the United States was expanding further westward beyond the Mississippi. It was

An Indian trading furs for a gun, 1785.

in this area, the traditional "West" of literature and folklore, that firearms were to have their most significant impact (see Chapter 5). In 1803, the United States had purchased from France most of the land between the Rockies and the Mississippi—the Louisiana Purchase. Land claims resulting from this sale, together with territory ceded by Mexico as a result of its losing the War of 1846–1848, made the United States' continental boundaries complete by 1850.

Conditions on the Great Plains seemed to resemble those that had existed in the East earlier, but this was not the case. Although the Plains were "undeveloped," the land was already clear, thanks to nature. Vast open spaces allowed one to hunt and travel by horseback. Cattle and sheep-ranching were possible, along with large-scale farming. Wild animals, particularly buffalo, roamed the fields, and bears inhabited the mountains.

Given these conditions, it is not surprising that the great eastern gun—the Kentucky Rifle—should be found wanting in the Plains. The Kentucky had been designed to kill animals that were relatively small and usually presented themselves as individual targets. Such game generally could be brought down by a single shot and was often hampered in its movements by the rugged terrain and thick forests. On the Plains, however, animals often traveled in herds, out in the open. A mounted hunter did not have the time to stop, dismount, and slowly load his Kentucky with its ramrod, not if he expected to hit anything. Furthermore, the relatively small lead-ball ammunition the Kentucky used was not powerful enough to stop the big game of the West—the buffalo, the elk, and the grizzly bear. Finally, people on the Plains led a rougher life, and guns were more likely to be mistreated there than in the East.

In response to the growing need, the Plains, or Hawkens, rifle was devised. (The latter name is derived from the two St. Louis brothers who perfected the weapon.) A muzzle-loader made primarily of iron, this new gun lacked the range of the Kentucky but made up for it in firepower. The Plains rifle was constructed shorter than the Kentucky rifle, so that it could be carried more easily on horseback. Also, its stock was made thicker, to enable the gun to withstand harsh treatment. All Kentucky ornamentation that stuck out and could thereby become caught on horsegear or clothing was eliminated, as was the use of brass, which could reflect sunlight and thus give away one's position. Since the Plains rifle was designed to fire large, heavy bullets, the weight of the gun was increased to absorb the greater recoil and to assist in aiming. The bore was also increased and strengthened to withstand the powerful charges of black powder sometimes set off in the barrel. Finally, the arm was equipped with a new form of lock, the "percussion," in which a hammer struck a priming cap, causing an explosion that set off the powder and expelled the projectile inside the barrel. In some respects, the system worked like a modern-day toy cap pistol.

The Plains rifle was used by western pioneers and also by a new breed of trapper-traders called "mountainmen." The latter, using pack horses to pursue game that had to be trapped or stalked, often engaged in lengthy hunts far from civilization. Constantly in danger from either wild animals or unfriendly Indians, the mountainman kept his Hawkens by his side at all times. In addition, he usually carried a pistol or two as personal protection for when his rifle was out of arms' reach. In fact, the average mountainman was literally armed to the teeth, with firearms, ammunition, and knives.

[23]

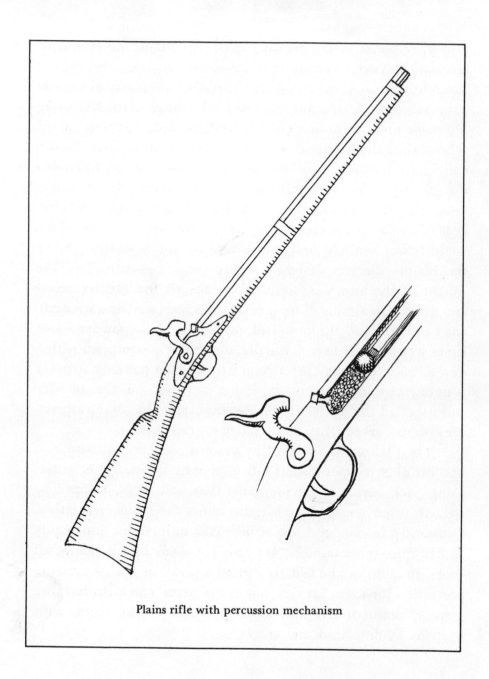

Plains rifle with percussion mechanism

Mountainmen were often the first to explore new territory. The military (the "cavalry") were usually not far behind. But they were so often confined to the forts they built in the wilderness that each pioneer realized it was up to himself to enforce the law. Physical strength and shooting ability were what stood between the mountainman and the great beyond. So vast was the area to be protected, and so few were the lawmen to do it, that in 1849 Congress authorized the sale of surplus army weapons to settlers in the territories recently acquired from Mexico. This sale is significant in that it was the first time surplus weapons were sold to civilians, a practice that continues down to today.

While settlement was occurring on the Great Plains, Americans also were leaping across this area and settling on the West Coast. There, cities were growing up overnight as a result of the gold rush of 1849 and the newly developed trade with Asia. Civilization in the true sense did not necessarily follow as quickly. Stories of street crime, personal violence, robbery, and so on during this period are like those one finds in today's newspapers.

In fact, resorting to the use of a gun was a common practice in cities on the fringes of frontier society. There were no city police forces, and each person was expected to defend him or herself. Occasional outbreaks of mob violence further contributed to the atmosphere of lawlessness. So accepted was gunplay that it was usually punished by only a small fine and a warning to do it outside city limits next time.

As on the Plains, there was the need for a new weapon, in this case one uniquely suited to the urban environment. A small, light gun, easily concealed in one's clothing, and most effective at short distances was what was called for. The answer was the "pocket pistol." Although there were many types and variations of pocket pistols, two stand out as having had the greatest impact on American society: the derringer and the pepperbox.

Henry Deringer had been in the firearms business for years, but it wasn't until he developed his famous pocket pistol that his last name became a synonym for such weapons, even if slightly misspelled. His pistol was a muzzle-loader fired by a percussion cap. With barrels a mere 2 to 3 inches (5 to 7.6 cm) long and the total gun 6 to 12 ounces (170 to 340 g) in weight, it was small enough to be concealed in a pocket, the palm of one's hand, or the bodice of a lady's dress. Although the derringer fired only one shot, it was deadly up to 6 feet (1.83 m), and this was all that was necessary for face-to-face encounters. This weapon was so versatile that it found acceptance among Eastern gentlemen, California goldseekers, dancehall girls, bartenders, anyone in short, who expected danger at close quarters.

During its heyday in the latter half of the nineteenth century, the derringer often made history. It was the weapon used by John Wilkes Booth when he assassinated President Lincoln. Frankie shot Johnny with a derringer in the popular ballad of the same name. And it was a derringer with which Charles Guiteau killed President Garfield in 1881.

Accompanying the development of the derringer was the evolution of the pepperbox, so-called because it was said to

Above: three models of Colt pocket pistols dating back to the mid-1800s. Below: a pepperbox pistol.

[26]

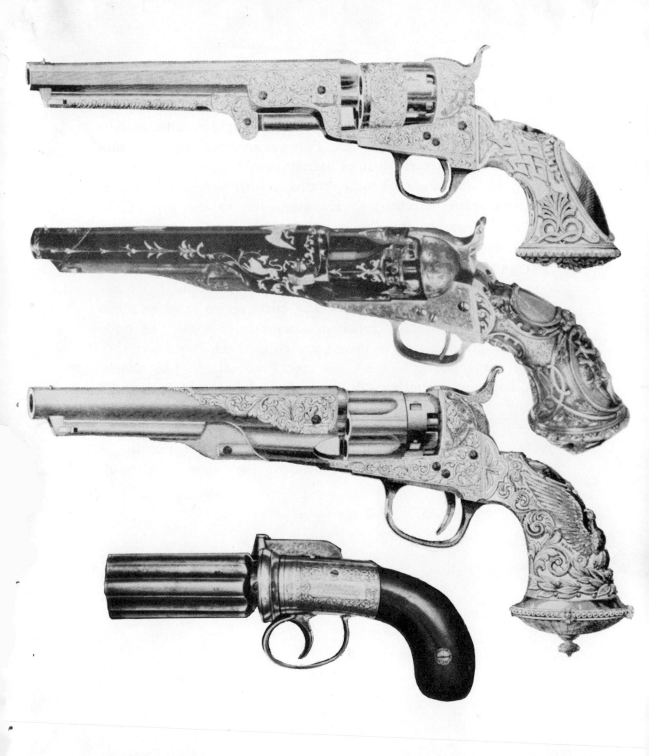

resemble canisters in which pepper was then stored. Like the derringer, the pepperbox was a personal weapon, varying from 3 to 8 inches (7.6 to 20 cm) in length. The unique feature of this pistol, however, was its ability to fire a multiple number of shots in relatively quick succession. This was accomplished by grouping together several distinct barrels, usually between three and six, and allowing each to be rotated in turn in front of the percussion-firing mechanism. However, due to the size of the barrel assembly and the fact that considerable pressure was required to pull the trigger and thus make the barrels turn, pepperboxes tended to be heavy and somewhat difficult to fire.

Nonetheless, the pepperbox still proved popular. Its low cost, multiple-shot capability, and effectiveness at close range made it a desirable weapon in a number of ways. The trade names given to some of these guns tell us much about how they were intended to be used; one model was called "The Ladies' Companion," another "Bolen's Life and Property Preserver," and still others "bicycle" or "picnic" pistols.

The pepperbox and the derringer were to become the favored sidearms in western towns and cities—until, that is, the "revolver" replaced them in the latter part of the nineteenth century.

CHAPTER

5

GUNS AND THE
CLOSING OF THE FRONTIER

The Civil War (1861–1865) marks not only a turning point in American history, but also a turning point in the development of firearms. Improvements in the design of shoulder arms, with the contributions of Christian Sharps, Christopher Spencer, and Tyler Henry, were particularly impressive. To Sharps goes credit for popularizing the technique of breech-loading, to the other two the acceptance of the idea of repeating fire.

The Sharps rifle first gained fame in the Kansas Territory of 1856. There, a local civil war was raging between pro and antislavery forces. Among those favoring the "free-soil" (anti-slavery) cause was a New York minister named Henry Ward Beecher. To assist his friends in "Bleeding Kansas," Reverend Beecher arranged to have them sent many of the new Sharps rifles. These rifles were packed in pine boxes labeled "Bibles," and when the anti-slavery people began to use these weapons they told everyone they were using "Beecher's Bibles." The nickname stuck.

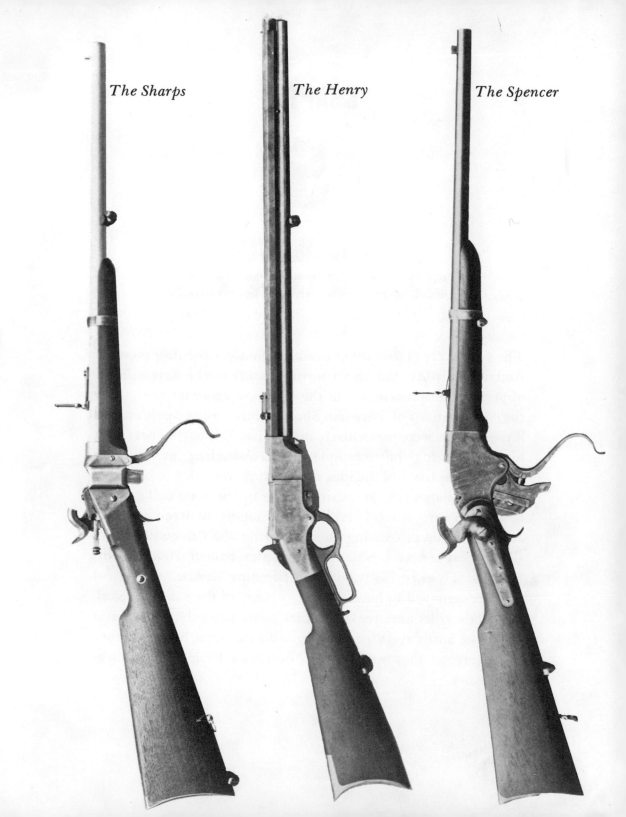

The Sharps

The Henry

The Spencer

Sharps rifles were also the reason for John Brown's famous raid on the Harper's Ferry government arsenal in Virginia in 1859. When captured by then U.S. Colonel Robert E. Lee, Brown and his followers had over a hundred of these guns in their possession.

It was their performance in the Civil War, though, that made the Sharps a worthy successor to the Plains and Kentucky rifles. The breech-loading Sharps was a considerable improvement over those rifles that loaded at the muzzle, particularly under conditions of war. Ammunition could be inserted without exposing oneself to enemy fire. (In using a muzzle-loader, one had to stand, place the rifle on end, and ram the charge home.) So impressive was the Sharps rifle, particularly in the Battle of Gettysburg, that people began to think the term "sharpshooter" was invented to refer to the accuracy one could achieve with this rifle, even though the term predates the gun.

Although the Sharps was an innovative weapon, it was the breech-loading repeaters designed by Henry and Spencer that signaled a true revolution in firearms. The Henry was capable of firing ten to twenty shots a minute, which meant it was at least five times faster than a weapon that had to be reloaded by hand after every shot. It was said that Confederate forces referred to the Henry as "that damned Yankee rifle that can be loaded on Sunday and fired all week." The Henry, and the Spencer as well, owed their capabilities to the development of the self-contained, metallic ammunition cartridge. No longer were bullet, gunpowder, and percussion cap separate items, nor were the first two loosely packaged together in paper. Now, all were firmly encased in a metal cylinder, which made loading easier for any gun with a breech mechanism, and introduced the possibility of cartridge "magazines" holding several rounds of ammunition.

Although the Spencer, with its seven-shot magazine and ability to fire up to sixteen shots a minute, was similar in operation to the Henry, it did gain one real advantage. In the middle of the war, Christopher Spencer was able to arrange an interview with President Lincoln. The President agreed to personally test the gun, was impressed by what he saw, and ordered that 100,000 of them be made by the federal arsenal.

With the end of the war, Americans could now turn their energies toward settling the vast area between the Mississippi and the Rocky Mountains. The technology first developed for the Sharps and Spencer was applied to more advanced rifles, most notably to the Winchester Models of 1866, 1873, and 1876. The Winchester name was to continue to dominate rifle production for the remainder of the century. It was these years, 1865 to 1900, that were to see the golden age of the cowboy, the last attempts by the Indians to resist white settlement, and the end of the frontier and many animals that had inhabited it.

If the settler represented the coming of white civilization in the East, it was the cowboy who portrayed this development in the frontier West. In discussing his role, it is important to separate myth from reality. The picture painted first by scores of dime novels, then motion pictures and television shows, has badly blurred the true image of this individual.

To begin with, one needs to remember that the cowboy was primarily a *cow* boy; in other words, his job was to tend cattle, and his gun was most often used in carrying out his job, much as the flintlock had been used by the early settlers. As one historian has observed, the cowboy wore his gun "in a holster attached to his belt as naturally as today's businessman straps a tie around his neck."

In tending cattle, firearms were used to control stampedes, to ward off enemy attacks by humans and animals alike, to kill stock that had become injured or diseased, and to shoot game for food when necessary. Guns also proved to have appeal as items of prestige, and were worn as dress apparel for social events, in hopes of winning the heart of a young lady.

The cowboy chose his gun carefully, since it was such an important part of his life. Working on horseback, it was natural that he should prefer a pistol to a rifle, due to the former's lighter weight, smaller size, and ease of handling. Although the pepperbox pistol was available, it had two disadvantages for the cowboy. First, it was heavy and bulky as a result of its many barrels. Second, since each barrel was like a loaded gun, there was the constant danger that more than one chamber would go off at once.

Both these problems were solved by Samuel Colt when he designed the first practical revolver. The Colt .45 had only a single barrel, behind which six cartridges were stored in a cylinder that rotated. As one cocked the trigger, a new bullet would line up with the barrel. The revolver could be loaded quickly and was almost sure to fire since it used self-contained metal cartridges.

The Colt possessed another feature that helped it gain popularity in the West—it was made with standardized parts. Up to this point, although guns tended to be similar, they were rarely identical. Thus, if something went wrong or broke, it was necessary to fashion a special piece to repair it. Each Colt revolver, however, was made to be a duplicate of every other, an accomplishment achieved by using the same molds each time. As a result, the elements of one gun were interchangeable with

Colt revolvers advertised in a catalog of the Old West.

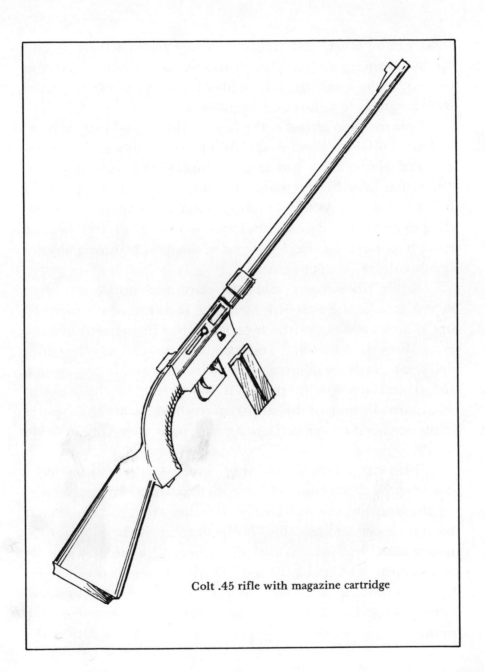

Colt .45 rifle with magazine cartridge

those of any other, and one could easily repair a broken Colt .45 by obtaining a spare part. This was particularly impressive to people who spent large amounts of time on the frontier, far from areas where a gunsmith might be found.

One common phrase of the day was that: "God created men; Colonel Colt made them equal." With the "six-shooter," the cowboy and frontiersman had at their disposal the great equalizer. No matter how big or tough the opponent, a Colt .45 could bring him down. As this weapon became a common way of settling disputes, the skill with which one used a revolver became more important, and has led to one of the most enduring legends of our culture—the gunfighter.

While "showdowns" did take place, and justice was often determined by one man with a gun, the West frequently pictured in the media did not exist. Often it was just the figment of some journalist's imagination. For example, instead of the slow, deliberate duels we so often see on television and in the movies, the typical gunfight in the West was a spur of the moment affair, usually started by drunken cowboys wanting to prove their manhood or get revenge against what they viewed as an insult.

There are other ways, too, in which this period has been distorted by nineteenth- and twentieth-century writers, such as by the image of the quick draw as being all-important. Wyatt Earp is reported to have told his biographer, "The most important lesson I learned was that the winner of a gunplay usually was the man who took his time." Obviously one had to be fast, but one needed to be accurate as well. In addition, the custom of cutting a notch in the stock of one's revolver to represent each person killed was *not* widely practiced in the West. Death was treated with as much respect as in the East, and few people wanted to brag about the number of men they had shot. Finally, while some men wore two guns, both were rarely drawn and fired at the same time. When more than one pistol was shown, it was usually intended to be just a display of firepower.

Nonetheless, it is true that the West during this time was developing so fast that law enforcement could not keep up. So, as in probably no other period before or since, each person became a law unto him or herself. In fact, so great was the legal void then existing that a relatively obscure man, Roy Bean, felt free to bill himself as "Judge Roy Bean, Law West of the Pecos." Everyone wore a gun, be he peaceful citizen, criminal, or sheriff. In addition to the well publicized "highwaymen" of the time, military deserters, bank robbers, and cowboys and mountainmen in town for a "good time" all were sources of trouble.

If civilization were to win out in the end, people truly capable of enforcing the law had to be found and supported by the local citizenry in the exercise of their authority. As one historian has noted, such individuals were characterized by "instant decision, fearlessness, swift action, and integrity to do the job." Given the conditions of the period, the last-named trait was undoubtedly the most difficult one to find. While state and territorial officers were usually straight and honest, local sheriffs and marshals often had shadowy pasts. The latter were hired primarily for their shooting prowess, and most communities were willing to forget the past as long as the man behind the star could protect the local inhabitants from outlaws. It was men such as these that Western writers later glamorized.

There is no denying the appeal of the gunfighter legend. Americans have gladly accepted as true the stories that depict

[37]

the heroism of men such as Wyatt Earp, Bat Masterson, Buffalo Bill Cody, and Wild Bill Hickok. To this day, toy guns continue to be one of the most popular items sold in American toy stores, and in a recent year accounted for over $100 million in sales.

Cowboys, frontier families, townspeople, and gunfighters in the post-Civil War period had one very important desire in common: they wanted to keep the Indians under control. This became difficult, partly due to the fact that the U.S. government was continuing to arm the Indians in a most thorough way, sometimes better than their own forces. As George Armstrong Custer, who in 1876 was to have his "last stand" at Little Big Horn, sarcastically observed, the weapons the Indians were using against whites were being obtained "through the wise foresight and strong love of fair play which prevails in the Indian Department."

The government justified its policy by saying: (1.) it provided payment for past injustices; (2.) it was necessary if Indians were to kill game in sufficient numbers to become economically independent; and (3.) it fitted into the new attitude of "paternalism" toward the Indian. Nonetheless, it did little to encourage peace on the frontier. Indians already had shown their ability to adapt firearms to their own mobile horse tactics. In fact, many Indians were capable of a feat that most whites would not even have attempted, namely, loading and firing a muzzle-loading musket on a horse at full gallop. This was made possible by the Indian skillfully pouring enough gunpowder into the barrel and then literally spitting the iron pellets in after it. (He had previously been holding the ammunition in his mouth!) Later, the Indians acquired large supplies of the new repeating rifles. As a result, the Indians, whose very survival as a people was being threatened by the expansion of settlements in the West, remained powerful military adversaries until the 1890s.

Ironically, however, it was the actions of civilians, probably more than those of the armed forces, that eventually doomed the Indian way of life. For in order to supply an immense demand for buffalo robes and other big-game products, professional hunters, joined by amateur "sportsmen," engaged in what probably was one of the most senseless mass animal killings in history. Men on trains hired to ride through buffalo country would shoot at the bison for fun from their parlor cars, and not even attempt to retrieve any part of the carcass for use. Buffalo shooting matches were held to determine the "champion" hunter. One such match saw Bill Cody kill 69 animals and his opponent, Billy Comstock, down 46 in an eight-hour period. The professionals collected over one million hides a year during the peak period of this slaughter.

Although some Americans bemoaned the passing of these herds, most did not. In fact the government had begun to realize, quite rightly, that the disappearance of the buffalo would mean the end of Indian resistance. As General Philip Sheridan noted at the time, Americans should feel grateful to the hide hunters, for "these men have done more in the past few years to settle the vexing Indian problem than the regular army has done in thirty years." It accomplished this by depriving the Indians of their chief source of food, clothing, and even the material from which their homes were built. It is not chance that the last Indian uprising (the Battle of Wounded Knee, 1890) took place shortly after the buffalo effectively disappeared from the Plains.

That same year, 1890, the U.S. government officially announced the closing of the frontier. America was increasingly

becoming an urbanized, industrial nation. Firearms were no longer really necessary to secure food or for protection against wild animals or hostile natives. Furs and hides ceased to be the important trading items they once had been. Yet firearms would continue to play a significant role in American society. As a growing world power and defender of the free world, it was necessary that the United States maintain and properly equip its armed forces. Thus important developments in firearms in recent years have mainly been a result of their use as military weapons. Some of these technological improvements have later been adapted in the manufacture of civilian pistols, rifles and shotguns.

Left: Buffalo Bill Cody.
Right: bison hunts, such as the one
depicted here, were nearly responsible
for the extinction of the breed.

CHAPTER

FIREARMS AS A MEANS
OF SPORT AND COMPETITION

As we have seen, the ability to shoot well was a distinct advantage to the early European settlers. It should not be surprising, then, that marksmanship was rated highly and that competitions among local citizens were frequent. The "shooting match" developed as a social event, which the entire family attended. One type, the "turkey shoot," has continued down to the present, though today's shoots rarely use live birds. In early America this activity generally involved a group of people shooting at a bound bird from a considerable distance. The first person to hit the turkey received it as a prize. Since part of the bird's body was often obscured by a log or tree, and the shooter stood some 100 to 300 yards (91 to 274 m) away, both speed and accuracy were necessary to win.

Early Americans also enjoyed shooting at targets. These activities could range anywhere from trying to drive a nail into a piece of wood with a bullet to seeing how closely together one could group a number of bullet holes on a sheet of paper.

Sometimes the sport involved shooting wild game in the woods, often squirrels. One variation of this was called "barking." Barking involved shooting the bark off a branch immediately below the squirrel, thus killing the animal by the concussion it would suffer in the fall. Another type of competition involved shooting birds in flight. (Hunters usually shot at birds standing stationary in trees or moving slowly on the ground.)

While marksmanship and shooting were generally practiced by men, many young boys were involved as well. The ownership of a gun became a badge of manhood, signifying that a boy had "come of age." As a result, a mystique grew up around the importance of having shooting skills. Theodore Roosevelt once remarked that "hardy outdoor sports like hunting are in themselves of no small value to the National character and should be encouraged in every way." Clubs such as the National Rifle Association have continued to foster this idea through the sponsorship of a number of marksmanship championships for men and boys.

Although sport shooting and recreational hunting were temporarily hindered by the growth of settled areas in the first half of the nineteenth century, they picked up momentum again with the development of the western frontier following the Civil War. In fact, one historian has called the years 1870 to 1900 the "golden age of hunting." It was a golden age for a number of reasons. First, game was plentiful outside of the metropolitan areas. Second, the war had introduced millions of men to the latest in firearms and many wanted to try them out in civilian use. Finally, the professional shooter, whether involved in hunting or in exhibition matches, gained great prestige as the American love of spectator sports began to develop.

This period also saw the emergence of the "market hunter," a man who killed all kinds of game for shipment to the eastern markets. Although there were some attempts to regulate this killing, most Americans believed that wildlife was an unlimited resource that could be harvested forever with no harmful consequences.

We know now that this idea was wrong. By the turn of the century, game was already becoming noticeably scarce. The passenger pigeon, which had once darkened the American sky, was almost extinct. The Labrador duck and the heath hen *were* extinct, and several other species, including deer, were becoming endangered. And the tremendous buffalo herds, once numbering in the millions, were all but eliminated by 1890.

Although national laws dealing with hunting would not come until around the time of the First World War, the threat of the total disappearance of American wildlife led to various early conservation efforts. A movement was begun in the last quarter of the nineteenth century, for example, to channel the sportsmen's efforts into the newly formed gun clubs.

Although a Swiss Rifle Club had been organized in 1853 in California, controlled match-shooting really began in the early 1870s. In 1873, the fledgling National Rifle Association sponsored its first marksmanship contests. A year later, to the surprise of the world, a group of Americans defeated the Irish Rifle Team, which had been champion of the British Isles. This victory did much to popularize match-shooting and advance the idea that the sport of hunting might be replaced by competitive, regulated contests.

However, the appeal of match-shooting was necessarily limited to expert marksmen. There still was a need for a sport that the average gun enthusiast could enjoy. In the 1870s and 1880s, "exhibition shooting" began to be a popular attraction at what were eventually called "Wild West" shows. Men and women such as W. F. "Doc" Carver, Adam H. Bogardus, Buffalo Bill Cody, Fred Kimble, and Annie Oakley became national stars.

At first, the targets used in these exhibitions were made of metal, cardboard, or glass. The last, in a ball shape, was frequently filled with feathers or some other material calculated to "explode" when a hit was made. In 1880, a Cincinnati inventor developed the first practical clay target. This quickly became accepted and led to the popularization of several types of clay target games including modern trap and skeet shooting.

However, the idea that such games would be sufficient to satisfy the hunting appetite of Americans was overly optimistic. Hunting live game remained popular. Therefore, moves began to be made to regulate hunting in such a way that opportunity would be provided for sport shooting and yet animal species would not be endangered and might even benefit through the thinning of herds in overpopulated areas. The result was a series of state game laws and regulations, and new government agencies empowered to enforce them.

Most of the hunting laws nowadays require the payment of fees for licenses that a person must obtain to hunt on public property. In addition, the federal government taxes hunting equipment and ammunition. The money raised goes into various forms of conservation, such as game management and the protection of certain forms of endangered wildlife. At the same time, "hunting seasons" have been established for different species of animals, and the size and number of animals that one

Above: Annie Oakley, of Annie Get Your Gun *fame.*
Opposite: a variety of Remington recreational and hunting guns.
From left to right: a deer gun, a duck gun, a target rifle,
a competition skeet gun, and a competition trap gun.

person can kill is regulated (the "bag limit"). Finally, the legal hunting season frequently lasts for only a small portion of the year.

As a result of such laws, some animals that were on the brink of extinction back at the turn of the century have made amazing comebacks. The eastern deer, for instance, is now estimated as being more numerous than it was when Columbus discovered America almost five hundred years ago! The survival of many other species, however, is still in doubt.

Today, there are approximately seventeen million sport shooters and hunters in the United States. One estimate indicates that over a billion dollars a year is spent on these forms of recreation.

Most of the opposition to hunting that now exists comes from individuals and groups who believe that it is basically wrong to kill any animal for sport. If game management is necessary, they say, it should be accomplished by nature and not by humans. Given our growing concern for the environment, this may well be an issue that will become more hotly debated in the years ahead.

CHAPTER

7

THE ART OF GUNSMITHING

We have become so accustomed to buying factory-made, standardized products, that it is easy for us to forget that when firearms were first produced in America, they were made by hand and were designed to fit the stature of the individual person who placed the order. Hours of painstaking work went into the production of a gun in those days, and the colonist expected to pay a top price for his gun. He also expected that gun to last a lifetime.

The fact that each gun was handmade, and that any replacement parts would also have to be so fashioned, put a high premium on producing a quality weapon in the first place. Since there was no guild system, or government approval or licensing of gunsmiths, each buyer had to trust to his own intuition and what he could find out in selecting someone to make his firearm. It is no wonder, then, that the presence of a master gunsmith in a community was highly valued. One had to admire a person who was both an expert metalworker *and* an expert woodworker.

While we have been using the word gunsmith in the singular, most firearms were produced by a small group of people, not a single individual. In addition to the smith himself, there were often partners, workers, and/or apprentices. However, it is important not to confuse this group with factory or assembly-line manufacturing. Each of the persons involved in the production of the gun was an artisan in his own right, and the finished item was always unique. Each worker was a specialist. One might be an expert in rifling barrels, another in making the stock, and a third in casting the pieces that composed the lock.

The process of manufacturing a gun was an extremely complex one, including the forging and rifling of the barrel, the making of the stock and the fitting of it to the barrel, the casting and assembling of the lock and the placing of it in the stock, the finishing of both the metallic and wooden parts of the gun, and the adding of elaborate designs and decorations.

In the days before there were machines that could bore a hole through a solid bar of metal, barrels began as flat pieces of iron and were formed into tubes. Two methods were popular. One involved preparing a rectangular sheet of iron, approximately the diameter and length one wished the barrel to be. This sheet was then heated until it was so hot that it could then be hammered into shape around a solid tubular rod, or "mandrel." The point at which the two ends of the sheet joined was welded together, hammered some more, and later filed down so as to be all but invisible. After the iron cooled, the mandrel was removed. The second method was a variation of the first, and involved twisting a long, narrow piece of iron around a rod in a spiral fashion. The latter method was felt to result in a barrel that was somewhat stronger and less apt to blow apart if an overload of gunpowder was inserted into the gun.

The next step in the process involved finishing the interior of the barrel. Since the bore had been intentionally forged smaller than desired, it was now possible to ream it out using a hand-operated bit on a lathe-like device. The purpose of this procedure was to create a completely smooth barrel and one that was "true," that is, straight. If the weapon was to have rifling, grooves had to be cut inside the barrel, which meant an extra step. By using a different bit, a steel rifling saw, and a spiral guide to which the unit was attached, grooves could be cut in the barrel corresponding to the ones that existed on the guide.

Two final operations were necessary to make the tube into a true gun barrel. First, one end (the breech), which would eventually be seated in the wooden stock, had to be closed off. This was done by inserting a "breech plug," a device which worked like a large, flat-headed screw, and therefore was unlikely to be expelled by the force of the explosion. Second, since these were muzzle-loading guns, some provision had to be made for igniting the gunpowder inside from the breech end. For this, a "touch hole" was drilled at that point where the lock would be joined to the barrel.

Now, the gunsmith turned to the task of fashioning the stock. The stock was always made from some type of hardwood, the choice depending on the gunsmith and the customer. The most popular woods were curly maple, cherry, and black walnut, although almost every other kind was used at one time or another. Care was taken to select wood that was thoroughly dried, which usually involved several years of aging, so that there would be no tendency to warp.

It was at this point that the real expertise of the gunsmith in the area of woodworking came into play. For while most men were capable of cutting the wood blank into the rough shape of a gun, it was only the true craftsman who could work the wood in such a way that the barrel, the lock, the butt plate, and the other metal parts of the gun would fit in perfectly and the total assembly would be pleasing to the eye as well. Gouges, chisels, knives, rasps, and sandpaper were all employed to handcut the piece of wood to size. One mistake meant that a stock had to be thrown away, for there was no way to fix it without building into the gun a possible point of future weakness.

The stock was now ready to have the various metal parts inlaid in it. These metal parts, including the lock, the butt plate, the ramrod pipe, the trigger guard, and the patch box among others, had been previously rough cast or forged, and then filed or ground into the proper shape. For their rough castings, many gunsmiths used the method known as "sand casting," an ancient process still employed by some craftsmen today. Patterns, usually sculptured from wood, were enclosed in a two-piece box (top and bottom) of sand. The pieces were then carefully separated without disturbing the sand, and molten brass was next poured in the sand "mold." When the brass cooled and hardened, it was withdrawn and then finished as described above. An alternate method was to forge the parts out of wrought iron and then "case harden" them by heating and immersing them in water, the result being steel-like pieces.

It was no simple process for the gunsmith to make sure that the lock, stock, and barrel all fit together well and in such a manner that the firearm shot accurately. There was always a considerable amount of fitting and shaping—remember that none of these parts was standardized, even though there were patterns.

While technically the gun as a mechanical device was now

finished, attention still had to be given to producing an arm that was beautiful as well. Often complicated and time-consuming efforts were applied both to the metal and woodwork to make the firearm a work of art. On the simplest level, the gunsmith might just stain the stock. However, it was not uncommon to have inlays of various kinds. Ivory, horn, brass, and even gold and silver were sometimes placed in decorative designs on the stock, and less commonly on the lock and barrel. Hearts, teardrops, stars, diamonds, crescent-moons, and fish were often used as motifs. In some cases, designs intended to ward off evil spirits or to protect oneself from enemies were placed on the gun. Pennsylvanian "hex signs" were common, as were "X" marks and fraternal symbols.

Not all design work involved inlays. Fancy engraving was also in demand. "C" and "S" scrolls, flowers, leaves, and shell designs were the basic configurations, although these were often combined in unique ways. Such work was usually limited to the metallic parts of the gun, with the inlays more commonly being set into the wood. Since these cuts were all made by hand, the gunsmith, who here was really acting as a silversmith, had to exercise great care that he did not make a mistake that might be impossible to hide. A variation of the scrollwork involved the process of "checkering," in which a design was created by carving parallel grooves into the wood at opposite angles, thus resulting in a series of small diamonds. Checkering had the added benefit of providing a better grip on the stock. Relief carving was also employed occasionally as well.

The final step involved "finishing" the firearm. Metal parts were usually treated chemically for the purpose of both enhancing the gun's overall appearance and protecting it against wear

and corrosion. Several techniques were employed, with the most prestigious being gold-plating. However, such a procedure was normally reserved for the wealthy, and the average gun was usually either "browned" or "blued" instead. Besides improving the looks of a gun, both of these processes protected the weapon from rust by chemically oxidizing the metal parts. The difference in color was caused by the chemicals used. Browning and bluing also minimized the glare that might result from the sun hitting the gun, and thereby improved the chances for an accurate shot.

The wooden parts, principally the stock, were also "finished." The most common method was to stain the wood dark by use of materials dissolved in aqua fortis (nitric acid). The result was a reddish-brown hue, which was highly valued and looked best on the curly maple wood that became so popular. Similarly, some guns were stained with a mixture of soot and oil. The wooden parts of the weapon were then oiled again until the surface literally shone. Great care went into the finishing of guns, since they often were a means by which a man's taste and social status were judged.

Top left: a modern-day apprentice gunsmith at work fashioning a gunstock in Colonial Williamsburg. Top right: in the Williamsburg gunshop, metal pieces are still mostly sand-cast. Bottom left: the craftsman at work in this picture is checkering a gunstock. Bottom right: finishing the stock.

As mentioned earlier, the production of firearms began as an individual or small group effort, often requiring weeks to finish a single gun. The Revolutionary War, and the subsequent establishment of government arsenals at Springfield, Massachusetts, and Harper's Ferry, Virginia, encouraged the growth of factory work and eventually from this emerged the great gun manufacturers of the nineteenth and twentieth centuries: Colt, Remington, Winchester, and Smith and Wesson. Machines were developed to accomplish more accurately tasks formerly done by hand, and new techniques, such as drilling the barrel through a solid bar of steel, were introduced. The new manufacturing methods lessened the demand for gunsmiths, as the new technology meant that a superior weapon could be produced at a cheaper price. As a result, today, the art of gunsmithing has become largely a hobby for a few.

GLOSSARY OF IMPORTANT TERMS

Ammunition—The combination of projectile (bullet, shot, or cartridge shell) and explosive charge (gunpowder).

Ball—The lead projectile used in smoothbore muskets.

Barrel—The hollow, metal tube of a firearm through which the projectile is expelled.

Bore—The hollowed out portion of the barrel of a firearm; also used to indicate the diameter of the same.

Breech—The rear end of the barrel.

Breech-loader—A firearm in which the ammunition is inserted at the rear end of the barrel.

Bullet—A type of firearm projectile, usually employed in a rifle.

Cartridge—A container that combines the bullet, primer, and gunpowder in one package. Since the mid-nineteenth century this container has been metallic; prior to that it commonly was paper and usually did not include the primer.

Charge—See *Powder*.

Derringer—A small, single-shot pocket pistol.

Flintlock—A mechanism in which a piece of flint strikes steel and produces sparks, thereby igniting the gunpowder and firing the projectile.

Hammer—The portion of the lock that pushes the firing pin into the primer.

Hand Gun—A firearm capable of being fired while held in a single hand, without the necessity for other means of support.

Lock—The mechanism that ignites the gunpowder and thus fires the projectile.

Magazine—A device attached to repeating firearms that holds a number of projectiles and feeds these into the barrel of the gun.

Mandrel—A metallic rod that serves as the form around which a barrel is forged and welded.

Musket—A shoulder arm, usually of smoothbore design.

Muzzle—The forward end of the barrel that has the opening.

Muzzle-loader—A firearm in which the ammunition is inserted in the barrel through the muzzle.

Patch—A greased piece of cloth or leather in which the ball is wrapped before being inserted into a muzzle-loading rifle.

Patch Box—A container built into the stock of a muzzle-loading rifle for carrying patches.

Pepperbox—A small, multiple-shot pocket pistol, which worked on a principle akin to the revolver.

Percussion Lock—A mechanism by which the hammer strikes a small, enclosed metal cup filled with primer and thereby ignites it and the gunpowder in turn.

Pistol—See *Hand Gun*.

Pocket Pistol—A hand gun of small size, capable of being hidden on one's person.

Powder—The explosive that expels the projectile from the barrel of a firearm when ignited; often used with the prefix gun-.

Priming (Powder)—A relatively small, highly explosive mixture designed to ignite the less volatile gunpowder.

Projectile—An inclusive term used to indicate any object (bullet, cartridge, shot, etc.) that is fired by the lock and propelled out the barrel of the firearm.

Ramrod—A wooden or metallic device used to push the ammunition into the barrel and to the back or breech of a muzzle-loading firearm.

Recoil—The backward movement (the "kick") of a firearm that results as a reaction to the firing and expulsion of the projectile from the open end (the muzzle).

Repeater—A firearm capable of firing a number of cartridges in quick succession without the necessity of loading each projectile separately.

Revolver—A type of multi-shot pistol in which a multi-chambered cylinder successively aligns a single cartridge with the barrel for firing.

Rifle—A shoulder arm designed with a barrel containing spiral grooves, the purpose of which is to have the projectile leave the firearm with a rotating motion.

Shot—Lead pellets used as projectiles in smoothbore firearms, such as the musket and shotgun.

Shotgun—A smoothbore shoulder arm, successor to the musket, which fires small, lead pellets called shot.

Shoulder Arm—A firearm of substantial length and weight that must be braced against the shoulder when firing; muskets, rifles, and shotguns would be examples.

Smoothbore—A shoulder arm in which the barrel is smooth, as opposed to being rifled.

Stock—That part of a firearm into which the lock and barrel are fitted and which supports the same while firing; the means by which a firearm is held, carried, and aimed; traditionally made of wood.

Touch Hole—The opening in a muzzle-loading firearm through which the fire is conveyed to the gunpowder in the barrel.

Trigger—A part of the firing mechanism activated by the finger that sets the hammer in motion.

[59]

BIBLIOGRAPHY

Buehr, Walter. *Firearms.* New York: Thomas Y. Crowell Co., 1967.

Colby, C. B. *Firearms by Winchester: A Part of U.S. History.* New York: Coward, McCann and Geoghegan, 1957.

————. *Musket to M-14: Pistols, Rifles & Machine Guns Through the Years.* New York: Coward, McCann and Geoghegan, 1960.

————. *Two Centuries of Weapons: 1776–1976.* New York: Coward, McCann and Geoghegan, 1976.

Colonial Williamsburg. "Gunsmith of Williamsburg." Williamsburg, Va.: Colonial Williamsburg, n.d. [film]

Dutton, William S. *One Thousand Years of Explosives: From Wildfire to the H-Bomb.* New York: Holt, Rinehart & Winston, 1960.

Ellacott, S. E. *Guns.* New York: Roy Publishers, Inc., 1965.

* Fenin, George N. and William K. Everson. *The Western: From Silents to the Seventies.* New York: Grossman Publishers, 1973.

Guns. New York: Wonder Books, n.d.

* Horan, James D. and Paul Sann. *Pictorial History of the Wild West.* New York: Crown Publishers, Inc., 1954.

Limburg, Peter. *What's in the Names of Antique Weapons*. New York: Coward, McCann & Geoghegan, 1973.

McNally, Tom. *Hunting*. Chicago: Follett Publishing Company, n.d.

* Monaghan, Jay, ed. *The Book of the American West*. New York: Bonanza Books, 1963. (See especially Chapter 7: "Guns of the American West," by Robert Easton.)

Nickel, Helmut. *Warriors and Worthies: Arms and Armor through the Ages*. New York: Atheneum Publishers, 1969.

Peterson, Harold L. *A History of Firearms*. New York: Charles Scribner's Sons, 1961.

* Rosa, Joseph G. and Robin May. *Gun Law: A Study of Violence in the Wild West*. Chicago: Contemporary Books, 1977.

Rosenfelt, Willard E. *The Last Buffalo: Cultural Views of the Sioux or Dakota Nation*. Minneapolis: T. S. Denison & Company, Inc., n.d.

Serven, James. *Two Hundred Years of American Firearms*. Chicago: Follett Publishing Company, 1975.

Tunis, Edwin. *Weapons: A Pictorial History*. New York: World Publishing Company, 1954.

* Waterman, Charles F. *Hunting in America*. New York: Holt, Rinehart & Winston, 1973.

* Wycoff, James. *Famous Guns That Won the West*. New York: Arco Publishing Company, 1975.

* Indicates books of a more advanced nature.

INDEX